THE LIGHT

Bonggani Sibusiso Maseko

Author's Tranquility Press
Marietta, Georgia

Copyright © 2022 by Bonggani Sibusiso Maseko

All rights reserved. No part of this publication may be reproduced, distributed or transmitted in any form or by any means, including photocopying, recording, or other electronic or mechanical methods, without the prior written permission of the publisher, except in the case of brief quotations embodied in critical reviews and certain other noncommercial uses permitted by copyright law. For permission requests, write to the publisher, addressed "Attention: Permissions Coordinator," at the address below.

Bongani Sibusiso Maseko/Author's Tranquility Press
2706 Station Club Drive SW
Marietta, GA 30060
www.authorstranquilitypress.com

Publisher's Note: This is a work of fiction. Names, characters, places, and incidents are a product of the author's imagination. Locales and public names are sometimes used for atmospheric purposes. Any resemblance to actual people, living or dead, or to businesses, companies, events, institutions, or locales is completely coincidental.

Ordering Information:
Quantity sales. Special discounts are available on quantity purchases by corporations, associations, and others. For details, contact the "Special Sales Department" at the address above.

The Light/Bonggani Sibusiso Maseko
Paperback: 978-1-957208-80-0
eBook: 978-1-957208-81-7

Contents

Preface 7
Acknowledgments 8
CHAPTER ONE Laying Necessities 1
    Part One Intelligence (Understanding) in Grounds 3
    Part Two Rousing Wording to Beginnings 5
    Part Three Assorted Initiatives 6
CHAPTER TWO A Test to Prune 8
    Part One   Awareness Is Knowledge 9
    Part Two   Knowledge (Good and Bad) 11
    Part Three Actions Worth Eternity 12
CHAPTER THREE The Path (Will) 14
    Part One   Unfold Your Soul 15
    Part Two Nurturing Effort 17
    Part Three   Complete Clarity 18
    Part Four Precept in All 20
CHAPTER FOUR Endlessness Is a Possibility 21
    Part One   Believe 22
    Part Two Wisdom 24
    Part Three   Love 26

    Subtle Lessons 28
    Necessary Lessons 29
    Informing Lessons 30
    Encouraging Lessons 31

Abstract

The words are conceived by situations that aim to structure a mentality into actions concerned about righteous values, as well as to react to the intention of being righteous.

May effort be inspired in accordance to various capabilities that ground our intentions to the Word.

Preface

Engaging my concern and ability to the phenomenon and program this book holds has been a journey characterized hardship, also effort, in adjusting immoral perspective intensely and purposely relevant and in line with time and also in determining accuracy in an acute manner that is assorted in value, when the future is accredited to prove quality, truth, righteousness, faithful, honesty, love, joy, honesty and patience, Being an instrument to fulfill and to be used in this process, I consider this moment my purpose, which is the will of the Word in me. Because if not for the Word, I would have not been able to be formed or to be. For him to be praised, honored, and glorified are what's only worthy to be present in me. He urges us to promote morality so that the present can be kind, and we can all be satisfied and contented with it

Acknowledgments

Firstly, I would like to thank the Lord of lords, God's mercy, and the Holy Spirit for giving my words such a true present to represent continuity as part of this reality. Moreover, thank you to the following participants' input: Prof. Thabo Israel Pudi from TUT and Coal City Courant news staff Michelle Mashiane. To my brothers and sisters and also to the elders from the house and church, for all their advice and words of encouragement to me that enabled me to stand my ground to achieve the end results of this book. I would like to thank the Xlibris team for assistance in copyediting, publication, in all, through making this book a success. Lastly, to the community of Emalahleni (Witbank), to my family, as well as to you-the reader-for without you, this book does not have value.

CHAPTER ONE

Laying Necessities

> **Summary**
>
> This chapter is based on exposing immorality in most situations we react to, get educated by, and discuss about. This chapter also implements definite wording as subject to the field of lessons required to nurture our consciousness, to elevate our sense of presence, and to inspire accurate options to consider.

Part One
Intelligence (Understanding) in Grounds

Once, when we were not part of a purposeful reality, we had our concerns on difficult conversations (evil) to discuss how we reacted toward living invented, deterrent perspectives in situations that inspire our intentions to create destruction. Complication-because of being unwary- is when lessons are supported and developed, resulting to hell being made visible. That causes misunderstanding to be effective, and on the other hand, the definite (morality) meaning is without value. Into righteous words come a simple definition to living life is, since such is in action, exposes a vital, intended reaction. And in a way, that is proven to be true though most find them not cooperative, the reason being those evil motives conceiving notions are believed and considered to be an important part of living while they are only a set in a series of darkness-hell. We are determined, as individuals in assorted understanding, and as it is, we are the reason why problems are there as well!

It is not only for our sake that we should be determined to approve, but it is the wise to be devoted to others' needs, which is the light most find to be puzzling to comply, and by failing, how can we then anticipate-also hope-to overcome our fears? As individuals, we should put in mind the importance of being present since it is a privilege and an honor to be blessed with- an honor that we, mostly, unwittingly know about, which causes us lost of understanding. And also because of flippant thoughts and attitude toward situations, we then prove our reality to not be worthy of our intentions. You are the Word's chosen messenger out of all souls, and only you are honored to be a distinguished bright view who possesses veracity.

Part Two
Rousing Wording to Beginnings

A sense that is durable in an extraordinary nature and preferable to a vacant notion that invention may proceed to result in grounds suitable as the furthest set of what is intended-we occupy such intentions within our personalities.

While it shows destruction as a challenge to conquer and to assimilate perfection that is part of us, it also shows a holy adventure and a necessary platform to rely on because without it, we are nothing. In general, about our indispensable welfare that is worthwhile for the sake of continuity, we must acquire an attentive sense subjected to an understanding that connects us with suitable lessons being words of wisdom spoken or read, for they are building blocks that structure our lives into a possible lasting moment forever and, with heavenly experiences, are attached to who we are. Perspectives have become so inevitable in living that we indulge in inculcating their grounds, which proves to us that existence is possible. And in an assorted state, we are described by, for instance, the professions; we are defined by our appropriate demeanors.

Part Three
Assorted Initiatives

As these lessons in action are incentives that we come to witness, they put in the effort, causing reaction to be the result and the fact that some were invented to be the result and others were invented to lead. It is when a dispute begins to infiltrate our world (understanding) in a way or when motives that differ from the real purpose decide to daunt our destiny into interesting cases and activities that result to an alternative result opposite to what our intention aims to achieve. Furthermore, about such set of misleading studies, character, and situations. They have their mark on being considered as well as being appreciated by superior to be practices individuals should let part in their reality (daily living). Such achievements have been approved by subtle methods; they are then caused to be understood.

To their grounds, those specific cases to be looked at and to be cautious about-as for their mass in our reality-are tremendous that they occupy almost every instance, being an issue. We are mainly governed by immoral behaviors and influences; this statement is supported by increasing types of reactions taking place and also the kind of characters living and developing within us. So how living should be supposedly destined depends on influences and motives-those that we are building our inchoate selves into as a start, meaning a situation in relation to your thoughts, behaviors, and the present that you begin to assimilate. Even your intention is without dispute and approval, as well as your consciousness. Moreover, for such conditions to be a success, it is an honor we are all deceived to witness.

Though we are influenced to behave in our unlikely ways, it is a strategy derived from the formula that resulted to the answer to complete us, where *understanding* is a term that consists of the power to attract attention and has been used to accompany misleading aims into living.

CHAPTER TWO

A Test to Prune

> **Summary**
>
> Since reality is based on knowledge, on this chapter, clarity on procedures influencing our behavior, lessons structuring a mentality that is compulsory, and a strategic criterion used as input that is advantageous to our present time are revealed.

Part One

Awareness Is Knowledge

Such tendency (awareness) has a lot of influence in situations. We are concealed from identifying synthetic and genuine knowledge between these situations we are part of. It is a problem in discussion that every individual is facing, and we all then need to be kept aware of them and to also begin structuring ways and methods that will be effective in availing and eradicating the meaningless intentions we are affected by. To begin with, start on conforming to the previous situation and know that addiction can be possessive. For us to be educated about the possible dangers and other information concerning what to expect, we must identify most of the acts we rely on and how willing we are to change.

Although words have the power to deceive our body into action, without you conscious taking part of it, it will result to nothing. Moreover, what is the reason why terrible circumstances exist? Lies within evil motives, wanting to make possible their will in our reality and then we become influenced completely. After all, the words' intention in us was, is, and would always be what our actions illustrate in the present that shows the real us. Since immoral ethics and behaviors were then invented, they had much to do with (the meaning) what the possible aim is and what the reasons behind anticipation are.

Part Two

Knowledge (Good and Bad)

How most lessons are discussed and taught by present situations, statements, and demeanors aim to evince in an assorted manner—"the method matters." Notions that are part and that form the defining process and their basic intention-explained by good and bad-are the issues needed to be cautiously looked at and also to be dealt with.

The reason why these situations are possible is, we are victims individually. We then need to accept the fact that reality is the main intention for continuity to be in a normative sense that enables a single unit of sequence to favor our destined necessities. Being involved and devoted to a coherent set of situations and then studying enable us to practice our attributes within that invent the precept we are best suited to follow. Reality is our obligation that we mostly lack intelligence, interest, and imagination in. On the other hand, by being attached to such words in the process, we acquire an inherent essence of reality. Restricted actions we are in need of to be edifying and to be creating a determined environment, which is a wonder. We are satisfied to arrange as it means to annihilate and to be effective in our demeanors and also us to denigrate.

Part Three
Actions Worth Eternity

Moreover, we must commit ourselves to present thoughts and conversations that provide us intelligence with vital lessons, which are as well supported as a guide to our way forward without impediments. We should relate our personalities into every efficacy method's intention to become attuned to fundamental knowledge in action for distinct assimilation and with vacuous impressions. Our subconscious will automatically be indignant by being submissive to grounds words we have fixed our mental and physical states into. Being a believer is the reason why we are aware without getting involved in adverse conditions. All obsessions caused by self-devotion are in favor of the essential concept that living is invented and that ameliorating environment is a need.

Furthermore, imagine being in a state of behavior that is difficult to stop or end and you're able to control it while the reaction was in your favor-also done in a flawless manner. The decision for the above statement to be a reality is considered possible, and the view to such reality is revealed by having faith in righteous words that define your perfection well. Somehow most complications offend our destined journey and the answers we depend on to brighten our paths. These two types of instances become a reality because of the authority we handed over to them by underestimating ourselves and the decision to give ourselves to their processes as situations. Power-being the influence that words have toward actions and thoughts-remains and in a sense so puzzling to adapt to because of the fact that living is our improvement that we always work on to develop; also, our present is under such process (where our potential expresses characters as time passes).

CHAPTER THREE

The Path (Will)

> **Summary**
>
> This chapter is based on determining the reasons behind the inventions of our true nature and intelligence that associate us to our purpose and also grounding divine measures to describe our personality toward the present.

Part One
Unfold Your Soul

Inspiration proves to be what wakes and develops the previous situation into a much better one, and it can be concluded that only what you are best inspired in, in a flawless manner, is relevant to uplift and even take our ability to be showcased in other parts of the environment. The meaningful situations we are persuaded into and the manner in which the type of power being used to influence us should be considered- whether they are right or wrong- because that will result into meaningless intentions that our souls will be regretful of, meaning that in every situation we take part in or are part of, we always need results with sensible outcomes. So, we should be engaging our capabilities in justifying facts that feature acts we can relate to well. With such attitude, we are able to involve ourselves into less destructive situations. Furthermore, association with anticipant reasons is part of taking a step forward.

An individual is gladdened also by a difficulty that most find hard to discuss and, even, explain. It is a hidden matter with fortunate situations that can instill lessons of possibilities in a sensible individual and with words that equip a willing heart to acquire righteousness, endurance, faithfulness, honesty, and love. They become effective by being convinced and believing in who you are first and living your actions approving so. It is the reason that will help accomplish realistic attributes and reveal your true being as a valuable person with a purpose to free your thoughts, behaviors, and living situations.

Part Two
Nurturing Effort

Struggling to be or to reach our full courage (effort) is a main cunning, problematic issue and while we are because of perspectives also situations in living. With the value, or worth, as the main incentive that dominates our thoughts and desires with influential reasons that have meanings in our lives, we find it hard to live without; this is also because of situations being the matter that proves reality in the assorted view and methods. Only a worth encouragement is rated as topmost, which is an issue that is arguable but has a supportable base from evil will.

Furthermore, reactions are established in various methods, where only one is mostly preferable, though sometimes there are some, among all, like when one is inspired to react because of desiring to fulfill a statement for the good of love, friendship and family or in a manner where not only his or her need is fulfilled but for the need that includes many.

Part Three
Complete Clarity

Somehow, though it is a difficult fact for our intelligence to practice and understand that living is only a matter of helping one another and also being there for one another, we tend, as individuals, to define life by practicing and by being more into perspectives that grant so. It is an unwary method that makes creation unpleasant and confusing at the end of a situation that we witness and decide to be ignorant of because of the addiction our thoughts were exposed to. Compulsory words in action are a form that nurtures a neophyte's thought to realize and begin a possibility that is sustainable. In return, we put worth to our future indelible values when obedience is part of the word defining our attitude and conditions. Our acts will only be eulogizing that narrow path and indispensable destination we devote to-the outcome we all decide and hope for.

Non sequiturs are enticing matters we seem to be not aware of because we've vacuumed lessons without the necessary module that forms a definite personality since the structure that we define consists of principles. As it is confirmed to be appropriate, we have to commit ourselves because the reason that we are present is described by our reaction toward the present and in a manner that is accordingly. The fact that our faith is questioned is the reason most are unable to stand daunting views, which are difficult to practice. Moreover, believe is defined by a level of consciousness that surmounts fear in visualizing and being certain without options availed. It is a concealed mystery that is a part of us but is puzzling to discover because the experiences that occupy our thoughts are situations made up by our immature thoughts that brought about failure as a disadvantageous perspective and an opinion associating our thoughts with impossibility.

Part Four
Precept in All

Words can connect well within us and are necessary for our life to be a possibility. They were given all the authority to give power. Moreover, concerning the word power in every situation in reaction or ideas in conversation, it is only words that are possessive of such—how miraculous is that? If we try to understand that words hold the true purpose of our will, we, by doing so, become informed that we are precise in our talk, thought, and reaction-a choice being a decision influenced by knowledge that gives clarity to how important words are. The fact that our various purposes are words that are lessons forming our knowledge proves a lot, especially through what we do.

Everything is just because of words. Our destinies are defined by facts as words, giving proper direction. Though it so, most are deceived by emotions. To be alive is not only to be present but to be beyond that because what we do gives others a clear definition on who we are and how we want to be treated. So, it is very important for one to be informed of conscious reactions and words since define who we are. Our everyday presence is a lesson that aims to inform us.

CHAPTER FOUR

Endlessness Is a Possibility

> **Summary**
>
> In this chapter, we have related vital parts of the divine Word with actions to endorse who we are and to define, as a whole, what we do. And as this is the last chapter, it is aimed to emphasize the overall point this book holds.

Part One
Believe

Faith is a result of a vacant mind looking forward without thinking about others' situations, and we are possessed of such valuable possibilities in various means that are flawless. Our burdens-their understanding in us, —create an indelible gesture that fixes its will in us as to how we're supposed to be. We then lack faith that proves docile to us in fulfilling intentions that denigrate and demean necessary grounds to complication because such acts are against that which results in conflicts and situations that disapprove of destined living. In contents, we, as individuals, occupy our unique personalities and understand how they possess steps and reasons that lead our actions to appropriate understanding in living and suiting our purpose well. We then begin to invite a constraint that curbs our desire by proposing statements and acts that are full of deplorable, despising senses in hand.

So how we decide to associate ourselves with desirable situations we are curious about has always cost us and filled our mental capacity with unnecessary memory and experience. Also, as that is the case, it then infiltrated inchoate and equivocal contentions that are not secular to what our necessity is. Moreover, when putting such views into practice, we find out what they inspire, intend, and mean; this is a controversial process that devastated our thoughts toward veracity. Also, our perspectives conceive opinions into grounds that aim to devour our true being- us.

Part Two
Wisdom

Way of living is described by the compatible situations we come across as individuals, though how unusual in our senses the fact is and that being resulted by uninformed approach of flippant this is the reason why we cannot realize our full, competent satisfaction as something conspicuous as they have to give a definable reason to why we are who we are.

Instances are present as well situations we related to in favor our intend and theirs in content manner. The capacity of words being availed, expressed, and defined in situations that are a complication is an unclear issue; such words being accompanied by a remorseless consciousness are notable. By being devoted, we then procure a stable reality with set rules, standards, and behaviors that are suitable. All in all, what defines our intentions, in an opposite fact, are the situations we take part in. By characterizing opinions, we were taught because of influential reality as our reward, there are situations we promulgate without knowing so. Being ignorant in an erudite method will reveal erroneous ideas and information that fabricate a process, making us distressed. Evincing for a good purpose is a moral act that is impenetrable from our thoughts and realizations because of the tendency of our thoughts to duplicate every idea presented upfront.

Part Three
Love

Such demeanor based on false ideas but are believed. Moreover, the word obscure is defined as a considered process that holds important values to our attributes. Denigrating statements get extreme attention from us since they provide us with a sense that is noticeable and because they equate the opposite of what we desire in with what we would usually do in an inaccurate manner that proves and gives in an efficient way preferable as far as our reality is concerned. As to liking personalities and attributes, we depend on and also have based our knowledge and values on being organizations that were developed from our experiences and environmental reality from past and present generations. These did result in formidable facts that are coherent for future humimito be preserved as they play a big role in nurturing and, also, edifying neophytes.

Although it is so, the fact that it's vital to our living. Fallacious obscure intentions are outcome behaviours formed by oblivion attitudes we occupied while we were unwittingly of our ignorance. Who we are, as a faculty or as a process, is described by a set of a series of challenges to learn from, as well as to be put into words to be a study? And for this reason, we were convinced to follow the procedures in order to create and to also become a disciplined society that will be based on principles and values. Our present inaction is an incense we depend on for our souls to be sealed with eternity and our reaction. The intention of persuading the process is the resource determining our true being. May realizations engage the views of those who still wander in the dark as the word begins to establish immoral situations that aim to eliminate evil intuition by infiltrating and networking information on the veracity about present and the future reasons.

Subtle Lessons

- So how living should be supposedly destined depends on influences and motives—those we are building ...

Page 12 (line 8- 13)

- How most lessons discussed and taught by present situations, statements, and demeanors ...

Page 18

- Our living is described by the compatible situations we come across ...

Page 35

Necessary Lessons

- The fact that our faith is questioned is the reason most are unable to stand daunting views, which are difficult to...

Page 29 (line 8- 11)

- Our burdens-their understanding in us—create an-indelible gesture that fixes its will in us and as ...

Page 33 (line 4-11)

Informing Lessons

- Though we are influenced to behave in our unlikely ways, it is a strategy derived from ...

Page 13

- The reason why these situations are possible is, we are victims individually ...

Page 19 (line 7) to page 20 (line 1)

- Moreover, believe is defined by a level of consciousness ...

Page 29 (line 11- 18)

- With the value, or worth, as the main incentive that...

Page 25 (line 4-12)

Encouraging Lessons

- Compulsory words in action are a form that nurtures a neophyte's thought to realize and begin a possibility that is sustainable ...

Page 21 (line 10-17)

- Non sequiturs are enticing matters we seem to be not aware of because we've vacuumed lessons without the necessary module that forms a definite...

Page 29 (line 1- 8)

Note	Date

www.ingramcontent.com/pod-product-compliance
Lightning Source LLC
LaVergne TN
LVHW040203080526
838202LV00042B/3301